Domination Basics
Secrets of the Alpha Male Book 1
by Drawk Kwast

I0425069

Drawk Kwast | The Alpha Male Advantage
Reality is a crutch for those lacking enthusiasm and imagination.

Published by Drawk Kwast Holdings, LLC
3565 Las Vegas Blvd. South, Suite 241
Las Vegas, NV 89109
www.drawkkwast.com

Printed in the United States of America on acid-free paper.
ISBN: 1-4538-0189-8
ISBN-13: 978-1453801895
Library of Congress Control: 2010915248
©2010 Drawk Kwast Holdings, LLC

Contents

Introduction

In every generation there are two groups…

There are the masses. For them, the world is chaotic and painful. They live most of their lives knowing something is wrong but not knowing how to fix it. Their battle cry is one of weak mediocrity. They are neither satisfied nor rested. Their biggest fear is that they will die nothing more than the sum of their failures and frustrations.

There is another group. They are the elite, the Alphas. They understand the universe as an equation. They get it. They are free in all the ways that others are not because they are free of fear. Everything is in abundance for them. They have the friends you want. They have the jobs you want. They have the cars you want parked in front of the houses you wish you owned. They experience the life you want while surrounded by the women you want. All the things you dream about, they know how to get - easier, faster, and smarter than you can. At the end of every day, they sleep with ease, looking forward to the next day's adventures.

Which group are you a member of?

What if you had a choice?

Domination Basics Part 1
Social Basics

Hey, we've all been there. It's Friday night. We've waited all week for this. We are looking good and are out for some socializing. But mostly we are out because we want to meet cool people. We want to make friends with cool people because we understand that we are products of our environments. The cooler, more successful, and more affluent our social circle is, the more we tend to get out of life. There is the ladies' man we would like to know, hoping that some of whatever he knows rubs off on us. There is the guy who always knows where the party is yet never stands in line to get in, and the guy who has all the connections who never seems to pay full price for anything. You know who these guys are. Then there is the good-looking girl who, by some stroke of fate and luck, actually seems to be interested when you talk with her. It's at that moment that it happens, out of nowhere, like a tsunami wiping out a small coastal village. As you get your chance to make a quality connection with someone, you say something dumb. Maybe you do something dumb first and then follow by saying something classically dumb. Either way, you know when it is happening, because you feel your value escaping out of you like a balloon deflating with that "phh-thhhhhhh" sound.

Everyone knows the solution is simple. Don't do or say anything dumb, ever. That's great advice, except for the fact that it's impossible. Sure, you should work on saying and doing fewer dumb things. As Smokey the Bear says, "Only you can prevent forest fires," but keep in mind that no one is perfect. Through Social Basics, we learn the core concepts used to keep social interactions running smoothly and the methods used to quickly put out fires when they arise.

We'll start off with three core concepts. The man who has mastered these concepts is prepared to walk into any social situation with ease. The first concept is to start off assuming that you have higher value than the so-called "cool people" you associate with. The second concept is that people will test you, even if it's just for fun. The third deals with how you choose to see your world and how strongly you hold onto those beliefs.

After you understand the core concepts, you will discover the methods to deal with challenges as they arise. These methods have been divided into three groups: Value Flipping, Interrupts, and Perceptual Flexibility. We'll look at the equation each uses and why it works, and then I'll give some examples of each.

It's worth mentioning that all of the examples in this book actually happened, and the methods have been repeatedly used in public by me personally.

Value Assignment

Let's start off with the value you assign yourself in relation to those you meet. When you are not interested in spending time with certain people you see, it is for a reason. You do not see them as having anything you want or want to be around. In this case, you assign them a label of having less value than you. This concept makes perfect sense to everyone. Who would want to hang out with boring people who are both socially and financially bankrupt?

Now let's look at the cool people whom you do want to be around. When you identify someone with something you want or want to be around, you have assigned this person value. The key to this value assignment, however, is that it exists only in your head and is not a real tangible item.

I am at a nightclub. I am sitting at a table by myself, close to the entrance. I see a man walk in with two young and attractive women. He is not that attractive himself, balding, and old. In response to what I see, I make an assumption that he has quite a bit of money, more than I do, so in my own head I assign him higher value than I give myself. The girls must be with him because he is rich (takes them out and buys them things). This

assumption may or may not be true, and most
importantly, this guy has no clue yet of what value
I have assigned to him in relation to myself.

People have no idea what value you have assigned
them until you start interacting with them.
Furthermore, people have no clue as to what value you
assign yourself until they start interacting with you.
However, in the first few seconds that you become
aware of each other, the puzzle pieces start
materializing at an alarmingly fast rate. It happens
much faster than you think.

Ever play poker? The cards are dealt. All the
players look at their cards; you see yours but do
not see the cards of the other players. In reality, it
is not even knowing the exact cards the other
players hold that is so important, but rather if their
cards are of higher value than yours. What is the
trick to playing poker? Being able to control your
reactions to seeing your cards and being able to
pick up on small cues displayed by other players
that may indicate the value of the cards they hold.

Like poker, the game we are playing is more about
self-control and perception than about the actual cards
you are holding in life. Perception is ALWAYS of

greater significance than fact, and facts cannot be
known without perceiving them. **Perception is reality.**

Have you ever been insulted by an idiot? Think
about this for a second. If the stupidest person on the
planet tells you that you are doing something dumb, do
you pay much attention to him? Probably not: after all,
what does he know? Similarly, if the biggest dork on
the face of the earth tells you that you are the coolest
person he knows, how excited will you get? Not very.
What does he know about being cool? Nothing.

> *Simple Thermodynamics 101: Is it possible
> for a piece of metal at a temperature of 100
> degrees to heat a colder piece of metal to 110
> degrees by simply touching it? No. Sadly,
> however, it is possible for a colder piece of metal
> to bring down the temperature of a warmer piece
> of metal by simply coming in contact with it.
> People are like pieces of metal, and temperature is
> like value. As they said in that martial arts movie,
> "You must understand this at your core,
> Grasshopper, before you will get your black belt in
> kung fu."*

Now here is the best part. Even though the
example above holds true to the social value we are
talking about, the temperature you pick for yourself is
totally arbitrary because you can control the warmth

you give off. With practice, you can be hot all the time. No one will be able to cool you off, and you will warm those around you.

Let's go back to our friend from the nightclub example above... It's time to actually meet him. But wait; before I do, I am going to get a little more information about him. I find out this guy has less money than I and has been saving up for the last five months to rent the two prostitutes he is with right now, and before tonight, he was a virgin. Now let's say I meet him when I accidentally spill my drink on him. Do I feel as stupid as when I thought he was a millionaire who had orgies with models every Friday night? Nope.

Why is it the nature of most people to start off by assuming that everyone has more value than they do? It's simple. People do not advertise their shortcomings to the extent that they advertise their strong points. You know all of your shortcomings, but when you meet a stranger, you see an advertisement for the good things about them while they hide their shortcomings from you. In other words, if you stopped dwelling on your own faults and could see everyone else's faults, you would assign value totally differently. Everyone has fears, failures, and frustrations that you do not see. Start from a more neutral ground. Recognize that when you see people with something you want or want to be around, you don't know all the negative stuff about them. Humanize them rather than putting them on a pedestal. More than you will ever believe, people are just people. The average person believes that he is not average. It's just human nature. The reality is that you are not a unique snowflake and neither are they.

So why is this so important? Remember this when you say or do something dumb: All of the people around you used to shit in their pants and relied on their parents to clean their asses. The first time they had sex (assuming that they are not lying about their virginity, as a greater percentage than you think do), it lasted less than a minute and was about as far from "good" as anything could be. By the time most people gather wealth, they have forgotten how to have fun. I could go on and on. Nothing is that big a deal. People make things a big deal. Don't participate in making things a big deal. Participate in making things enjoyable, first for yourself and then for others.

Tests

Now let's move on to the second concept, that people will test you.

I once met a girl who was incredibly attractive by anyone's standards, including her own. This girl would play the cutest little game with men on the first date. She would wait for them to make a statement, and then she would come up with the most uncomfortable reply she could. The guy would say that he is rich, and she would say that she respects guys who starve to death as they create their passions in art. Another guy might say that he has a Lamborghini, and she would get upset with him for helping to put a hole in the ozone layer with a car that gets nine miles to the gallon. If a guy said he was a health nut, she would tell him that's stupid because everyone is going to die and he is missing out on pizza. It didn't matter what the guy said. She was a Polarity Responder. She would say the opposite to see him squirm and change his story to fit her views. The poor bastards never figured out that the only way to win with this girl was to not care. So what kind of guy made it into her bedroom? The one who was strong enough to not play her silly little game.

Don't be the overly apologetic type. It's annoying. If you actually made a mistake, apologize quickly, fix it quickly (if you can), move on, and get everyone giggling again. If you truly believe you did nothing wrong, do not apologize for your actions. You can apologize for how they feel about your action, but **never apologize for what you did not do wrong.**

I met a guy at a bar once while I was talking to his sister. He asked me to hold his beer while he went to the bathroom. I asked him how long he would be gone. He said no more than five minutes. I agreed. After twenty minutes, it was time for me to go dance with his sister, and he had yet to return. I threw his beer in the trash and took his sister to the dance floor. About ten minutes after that, he walked up to me and asked where his beer was. In the trash is where it was. He then asked me if I was going to buy him a new one. I used one of the easiest words in the English language to speak (yet an alarming number of people have difficulty saying this word): no.

About a week later, I bumped into him at a house party where I was with his sister. I walked over to him as soon as I noticed him and offered a fresh cool beer, welcoming him to the party. We have been friends ever since. You see, he figured out that I was no one's bitch, and in reality, I did give him his beer back. In fact, I threw out a Budweiser and gave him a Heineken. Turns out he approved of his sister dating only guys who knew how to handle themselves (and thus were able to keep his sister safe). It was a test; I passed. His sister was an acrobat in bed, the reward for passing a test like this.

BOTTOM LINE: Don't completely crumble at the first sign of a little tension. Show them that you have some substance to you.

Reality Projection

We get the last concept from Neuro-Linguistic Programming (which is a set of techniques whose goal is to alter limiting patterns of thought, behavior, and language). In NLP, there is a term called *frame* and a concept called *frame control*. A *frame* is a metaphor for how people see their world. You can think of it as a window frame through which you see the outside world. Or you can think of it as a frame around a picture. Depending on the style of the frame, you see the picture slightly differently. If you put an expensive frame around "art" created by a two-year-old and hang it in an art gallery, chances are that everyone who sees it will think it's expensive. It's silly, but this holds true for the real world. Remember, perception is always more relevant than fact.

What we are talking about in this section is your ability to project your *frame* (how you see things) onto others. Effectively projecting your reality results in your reality becoming everyone else's accepted reality. Or in other words, the strongest *frame* always wins.

Adolf Hitler – Master of Reality Projection. This maniac manipulated the resources of an entire country into killing a few million people at his discretion. As soon as Hitler killed himself, the whole country flopped to yeah, not so much, and the power of the Nazi organization went bye-bye instantly. He would have made one hell of a used car salesman!

Or we can look at the classic "nuh-uh" argument used effectively by six-year-olds and (even more effectively) by the Catholic Church. When the first person declared that the earth was round, the Church said "nuh-uh," and everyone went with it. You would have thought that people learned their lesson, but when someone later declared that the earth actually revolved around the sun instead of the other way around, yet again the Church responded with "nuh-uh" (a very impressive logical argument used for the second time) and declared blasphemy again. The people of the Church went along with it again. Silly people. It never fails to amaze me that people are most comfortable following someone else as long as everyone else is doing it, even if it defies science and logic. Just amazing. Never underestimate this power.

Have you ever heard that sane people will sometimes question their sanity but the truly crazy are sure they are sane? The crazy people will hold their frame, *and no logic or proof will change their minds. Normal people question their reality.*

Therefore, you have the opportunity to repaint it for them when they do.

Did you know that if you use the "hang loose" hand gesture from Hawaii in certain countries in eastern Africa, you might have a spear thrown at you because it's an incredible insult there? Actually, what I just said may or may not be true. It's not true. Actually it is; it's a weird and true fact, and after my last example, I figured that you might expect me to try to lie to you, so I picked something true that would sound false. In reality, this is total bullshit. OK, no, it's completely true, but until you look this fact up on Google, you are not going to believe me. It doesn't matter either way. It's not important. So why are you wondering about this? Because you are probably, for the most part, sane, so you have doubt. You will learn to use this concept with great effectiveness later on in this book (no, really, the thing with the gesture is true, or maybe not).

Now with the core concepts out of the way, let's get into the good stuff. The tools, tactics, methods, whatever you wish to call them, are: *value flipping*, the *interrupt*, and *perceptual flexibility*.

Let's pause for a moment first and look at the above paragraph. Did you notice how it lacked the power that seemed to be a common thread throughout all of the paragraphs above it? The reason is that I left the categorizing of what we are about to discuss up to you. I labeled my uncertainty rather than the topics and therefore projected a weak reality when I said "tools, tactics, methods, whatever you wish to call them are…" This leaves you thinking, "Wow, this guy is supposed to be teaching me something that I do not know, and he is now asking me to categorize what he cannot." Weak! You must choose and commit to your reality quickly (even if you are sane and unsure) and project it clearly, and then people will believe you because they are never 100% sure (unless they are crazy).

OK, moving on now to the methods. Just remember the above core concepts as you learn the methods.

Value Flipping

Any method that raises your value over someone else's value (and lowers theirs in the process) is *value flipping*.

Do you remember the first time you tried to argue with your parents? How did that work for you? What went wrong? Simple. Your parents knew that they held all the marbles. At that point in your life, everything you had came from your parents. As adults, we fall into similar value seeking habits with strangers. We want to be liked, so we watch others for clues that they approve of what we are doing. If we start to feel like they do not approve, we adjust our behavior to get their approval. If we get the people around us to like us, maybe we can get other things from them. Again, look back to your childhood, and you will quickly see where this pattern started. This behavior worked great for you at age four, but in the real world, it hurts you.

FACT: People try to figure out where you are coming from and respond with the opposite of what you need.

Two men walk into a bank. The first man has only $87.03 in his account, just lost his job, and has no assets. The second man has over one hundred thousand dollars at this bank.

Additionally he earns a little over ninety thousand dollars a year as collected rent from the properties he owns. Which man is going to walk out of this bank with a loan? It's going to be the one who needs it the least.

Two men sit at the bar, one to the left and one to the right. The one to the right has recently married and is away from home on a business trip. The one to the left has never had a girlfriend and lives less than a mile away. An attractive single woman enters the bar. Now, if you had to wager $100 of your hard-earned money as to which man she will sit closer to, whom would you pick? I have tested this and found that women are more attracted to "taken" men (all other variables being the same), even if they are not told which one is taken. She will be more drawn to the person who needs her company the least.

We wish that the world did not work this way, but it does. I am not here to tell you about fuzzy, pink, floppy-eared bunnies that have just too much love inside of them. I am here to tell you all the things you wish you knew years ago about how things really work on this planet. The more you try to get approval from people, the harder it will be to get it. The more that you show them that you do NOT value their opinion (thus lowering their value) and that you care more about what you think (thus raising your value), the easier it will be to get their approval.

So how do you use this method to your advantage? Understand that the more you show this mindset before you say anything dumb, the less impact the dumb thing will have. The reason is that when others are trying to get your approval, you already have theirs. After you do something dumb, don't show people how much value you give them by overcorrecting. In fact, after you pull any bonehead maneuver, the method is to show that you see yourself as having more value than they do, and get them to see how. Here is the best part: you do not even need to be completely successful. As long as they stop to contemplate what you are saying, they have stopped thinking about what they think about what you just did. They may or may not go back to their original thought. That is a question of how well you control the situation. If they should respond by just laughing at your statement, great. If you have them laughing, everything just got better.

Practice this skill, perfect the ability to do it without insulting people, and you will be golden. Always remember that it's much easier to make friends with people who are not upset with you for insulting them. Sarcasm is saying something good and meaning something bad. Flirting is saying something bad and meaning something good. *Value flipping* is showing people they have lower value than you (or just getting them to question their own value) and having them smiling at you while you do.

Have you ever known a guy with a bratty little stepsister? How did their relationship work? He would always tease her and talk about how she bothers him. You would think that sooner or later she would just leave him alone, but she just keeps on coming back for more. She comes back because the less he cares about getting her approval, the more she is drawn to him. After a while, she is seeking his approval. Ironically, if anyone were to threaten this little girl, have no doubt that in an instant, he would protect her, and she knows it.

Be like this guy.

Value Flipping Examples

He says: You know, oddly enough, that only
             happens to me when you are around.

She says: Do you know what your problem is?
He says: Yes, and I bet you would have trouble
             pronouncing it.

He says: I'm out of my mind, but feel free to leave
             a message.

He says: Ah... I see the screwup fairy has visited
             us again. Lucky for me, she is the tooth
             fairy's sister, and I will have two dollars
             under my pillow tomorrow morning.

He says: I have plenty of talent and vision; I just
             don't care.

He says: Apathy is great, and if you disagree, I
             don't care.

He says: The fact that no one understands me
             means that I'm an artist.

He says:	Errors have been made. Others will be blamed.
He says:	Chaos, panic, and disorder – my work here is done.
He says:	Am I the only one who hears clown music in the background right now? Do you hear it when you screw up?
He says:	It's only fun if it's only fun for me (best said with a silly smirk on your face while clapping your hands together and bouncing slightly – repeat a few times).
She says:	What's wrong with you?
He says:	I keep a list. It's alphabetized for easy reference. Can you read?

The Interrupt

This method is like pressing the pause button, fast-forwarding, and hitting play again.

Have you ever heard someone say "don't change the subject" in the middle of an argument? Well, that would be an example of the other person in the argument attempting this method and failing. We are going to start off by looking at the extent to which people do this.

> *A man is arguing with his wife about how much money she just spent at the salon. She responds with "Why don't you love me anymore?" This is an interrupt. Her comment is completely logically disconnected; because men argue logically, he has no clue how to respond. He is lost and therefore just lost this game. She has interrupted his attack (and shown us that she has deep-seated emotional issues that have been building for a while).*

> *One of my favorite movies,* Real Genius *(1985), has a scene in it where the lead character starts hitting on a cute young woman. She responds by asking him if he can hammer a 10-inch spike through a board with his penis. He gets a little derailed. She interrupted his thought process.*

A man walks over to the most attractive woman at the bar and says hello. She responds by telling him that she does not talk to ugly men. He tells her that's OK, he wasn't interested in talking. He was interested in her buying him a drink. She has no response to that (what a curve ball) other than cracking a small smile. Smiling comes before laughing. Get them to laugh, and you can get them to do anything. Ugly or not, this guy knows that.

A man walks up to a complete stranger, says a few words, taps him on the nose, and next thing the stranger knows, he cannot remember the last three minutes. We get the term interrupt *from the Hypnosis/NLP world. This man is familiar with this world. Ever hear of the Jedi mind trick? He just did it in real life. It takes work, but with practice, your Reality Projection gets so strong that you can interrupt other people's reality. When you get good enough, they will forget their reality.*

So at one end of the possible list of results, you make them giggle a little and lighten the tension. At the other end, the more advanced end, they forget completely, and the tension disappears with their memory.

Interrupt Examples

He says:	Hello.
She says:	Go away, asshole!
He says:	Wow. You are spunky. I like that. What is your spunkiness based off of?
She says:	Huh? (She heard just fine – she has been interrupted and doesn't know what to say now, so she is buying time.)
He says:	(Holding his *frame* like a champion with a smile on his face still.) You have true strength. Where do you get that from? Are you a lawyer, diplomat, business owner? Do you volunteer for humanitarian work?
She says:	Ah, I have been drinking a little.
He says:	(Both of them laughing a little.) Spunky and honest! Wow. Can you cook? (Both of them laugh a little more at this point, and he wins. The rest of the conversation was easy – including the part at the end where she asked for his phone number. Believe it. It happened. I was there. Ever since, this is my default response to a bitchy woman.)

He says:	Did I just say that? Sometimes I do that when I'm not paying any attention to who I'm talking with. I was distracted by… (Point at something across the room and start talking about it.)

He says:	What are you, retarded?
She says:	Ahh… (with a little hurt puppy look on her face).
He says:	Did I ever tell you that my dad would drink pickle juice straight from the jar?
She says:	(Nothing)
He says:	Did you know that the Native American Indians called corn *maize*?
She says:	Yes.
He says:	I think that is a-MAZ-ing. Don't you?

She says:	(At a fast food place) …and super size it!
He says:	Are you on drugs?
She says:	Are you being a jerk?
He says:	Welcome back! Now that I have your attention, would you like to split a hot fudge sundae with me for dessert?

He says: Oh, look! Bright shiny thing over there.
            (Point in any direction and walk away
            immediately – come back later with a
            new topic of conversation.)

She says: (Doesn't matter – anything about men)
He says: Hey, I'm up here! Stop looking at me like
            I'm a sausage with feet. (Then start
            talking about your feelings.)

Perceptual Flexibility

If you truly believe that you are the coolest person in the room, then everything people say about you must be something good. That is what you base your response on. This method gets people to question what is going on. Usually, those who start questioning their reality are also the first people to start losing it. Once the door has been opened, so to speak, almost any idea can get in. If ever there was a how-to book on starting a cult, this explanation would be covered at great length in the first chapter.

Remember when I said that the crazy people will hold their frame, and no logic or proof will change their minds? Somehow, no matter what you say, they see things from their point of view.

There are **ALWAYS** different ways to look at the same situation. Figure out the angles, and pick the one that suits your goal.

It's a woman's right to choose because it's her body. Abortion is murder because it stops a beating heart.

The end justifies the means. The means are not justified by the end result.

People who believe in life after death spend this life working toward the next. People who do not believe in life after death think the others are missing out on a lot of fun that they are getting no second chance at.

The reporters ask the presidential candidates any question they want, and it seems that the candidates answer whatever question they want, even if it isn't the question they were asked. The reporter asks one of them if he is going to increase taxes and gets a response that because of the taxes on gasoline, we need to research alternative fuels. Ah, politics.

How could this be applied after you say something dumb? It's simple: You didn't say anything dumb. What you said was brilliant or comical. Oh, they thought you meant X? Silly them, you meant Z. Sure, you may get called on what you are doing, or maybe not. At worst, everyone has a little giggle. Have you ever seen a fortune-teller do their thing? That stuff is almost believable. They practice, and so should you.

Perceptual Flexibility Examples

She says: I'm thirsty… I think I want a drink.

He says: Oh, thank you. Um, Heineken for me, please.

She says: Nice shirt (sarcastically).

He says: I'm glad you like it.

She says: Nice shoes (sarcastically).

He says: I picked them up in San Francisco at a fashion market, and I've been getting tons of compliments on them.

She says: Can you stop doing that?

He says: Now you try.

She says: That is so annoying!

He says: Happy to keep you amused.

He says: (Gets caught staring at her breasts.) I just realized that you look like a grown-up version of my little niece Rebecca. She is seven years old and just the cutest little thing. (Then go into a story about her.)

She says: It's getting late.
He says: I'm not going home with you. I'm not
              that easy. Well OK, but you're going to
              have to buy me another drink first.

Keep in mind that everything you have just read is as much of an art as it is a science. It requires practice to get good at it. And as with any art, it requires a mixing of all the elements, along with your own personal flavor. As I'm sure you have already realized, the three methods work together, and in each one is a little of the other two. You will also realize that the three core concepts we started with are parallels of the three methods. What you have learned is simply one thing. In fact, as you read this, you may even feel these concepts and methods condensing and solidifying inside of you, right now.

One last thing to remember: socializing is fun. Keep it that way. Don't let anyone steal the smile from your face, as your goal is to make them smile. Keep it fun, and keep it playful.

Domination Basics Part 2
Business Basics

It's Thursday morning at exactly 10:03, and you are at the end of your presentation. You're doing what you do best. In fact, you may even find a little smile on your face. Your PowerPoint presentation and matching documents are vibrant. Your voice fills the room in a commanding yet calm way. You feel the vibe in the room and know that you are moments away from getting the final approval. Then like a piano string breaking in the middle of a concert, something goes wrong. Is everything lost? No.

I push people to find success past their self-perceived limits. You will find this point beyond your failures. True learning can only happen when you do not already know the answers and push yourself to find them. True success will be found in the experiences you have not yet had. This process never ends. You must stay in uncharted territory and learn from it. Always take things no less than 10% further than you did last time. That 10% is where the magic happens.

If you are comfortable making $24,000 per year, figure out what you are going to have to do to make 10% more next year. If you are making $100,000 per year, it's time to get out of your comfort zone, and figure out how to make 10% more. If you are making silly amounts of money already, it's time to figure out how to work 10% less, maintain the same income, and get 10% of your life back!

Now, I know what that little voice in your head is saying. It's correct. If you push the limits, even in the smartest and most calculated way possible as I teach, things will go wrong. Over a long enough time line, everything starts flying sideways. This is a fact that you must embrace. Focus on learning and abandon fear. Make mistakes quicker than everyone else, and you will learn faster than everyone else.

> *Two men are sharing a campsite. A bear comes toward them. Larry looks at Steve in terror and doesn't know what to do. Steve starts to run. Larry runs after him but exclaims that bears are too fast and they will never outrun the bear. Steve knows this. Steve also knows that he doesn't have to be faster than the bear, just faster than Larry.*

This is reality. Things go wrong. If you don't have anything going wrong, you do not have enough going on. We live in a world where the Internet has created such a wealth of information that the result is a poverty of action known as *analysis paralysis*. You must avoid the trap of paralysis from over-analysis. You will never be able to plan for every possibility, and trying to do so will only result in a lack of action. **Action is the only way to fail enough to learn and thereby learn enough to succeed.** Research enough to find direction. From that point, keep researching as challenges present themselves. Deal with every problem **episodically** and **pugnaciously**. Pause from reading this and look these two words up.

Business Basics is a guide for how to maneuver when things periodically and inevitably go wrong in the business world. Some may call this the guide to the "least painful way to learn when falling on your face." I would call it "the smartest path of what doesn't kill you makes you stronger."

The Scoreboard

You will remember from Social Basics that we focus mostly on how people feel about us. If we do something dumb like trip over our own feet, we make a comment about how that only happens when they are around. We think they are bad luck. They usually will laugh in response to that, and everything is fine. When dealing with feelings, there is no scoreboard to really indicate exactly where we are. It's all a little fuzzy. One of the things we do know is that if they are laughing, things just got better, but we don't know how much better. These things are true in business; however, we have one more additional and more important factor. It is very precise and easy for all to read. This factor is a scoreboard called money. At the end of the day, one thing is for sure: you will have a hard time getting someone to smile if you are helping them toward bankruptcy.

When I was 20 years old, I owned a business that sold equipment to schools. The good news was that I managed to secure some good-sized contracts. The bad news was that schools buy everything on NET 30 (meaning I get paid 30 days after I deliver the goods) and almost never pay their bills on time. The result was that I did not have the money to purchase the equipment from my vendor, who demanded payment at pickup. Most people would have seen this as a problem. I looked at it as a challenge I was about to learn how to overcome.

My banker introduced me to a person who was willing to loan me the money I needed to make the deal happen. I was young, so in his eyes he had a high risk, which meant obscenely high rates. I happily agreed because even at the high fees for the loan, at least I was able to do the deal. I was looking at the monetary scoreboard, and some points looked better than no points on the board at all. The deal was simple. He paid my vendor, and 30 days later, I was to pay him the loan back plus a few thousand dollars. If my customer paid me late, I owed my "loan shark" 1% of the principal for every day it was late.

On my first deal, the school paid 19 days late. I only had about 18% profit figured into that first deal. Most would say that I failed. I didn't fail; I learned something.

Did I stop doing business with everyone? No. That would have been stupid. I just paid a few thousand dollars to "learn something," and it would have been a waste to not keep on going and use that knowledge for next time.

After a few deals, I had a system. I had called down to the district accounting office, flirted with the girl who answered the phone for a while, and asked if it would be possible to pick the check up when it was ready. Amazingly enough, she said yes, and I had cut a few days off by avoiding the U.S. Postal Service. Then every time I came to pick up a check, I brought fresh-baked chocolate chunk cookies. Amazingly enough, the checks got cut quicker and quicker, and I never even had to call to remind them. I was rewarding their good behavior. I received one payment before it was even due.

I paid to learn the rules of the game. It became a very profitable game.

If you think the story above was about selling equipment, you are very wrong. I was selling fresh-baked chocolate chunk cookies. No matter how big your deals get, never forget the human element. Some people will tell you that "it's just business and nothing personal," but I am telling you that if you win over the people, you've already won the game.

Your Feelings Are Irrelevant

The next concept to grasp is that even though the feelings of the people you work with factor in, *your* feelings must be left out of the equation. You must choose to logically override your emotions in favor of getting things done. Remember that in business, we only keep score with money. Now, I am not talking about morality here. There is a simple truth in the universe that if you put out bad energy, bad energy will come back to you. What I am saying here is that you will make more money when you start doing one simple thing: learn to control your emotions.

One of the companies I owned in my early twenties was a computer consulting company. One side of that company sold tangible goods, and the other side sold services in the form of monthly service contracts. When I got started, I figured out fast that I had some clients I genuinely liked and others I did not, to say the least. Pain is the universe's way of telling you that you are in disagreement with what is. When you are in pain, any kind of pain, you have only two options. The first is to accept it. The second is to change things. The longer I live, the more I find that the first is reserved for only a short list of things like death and loss of a limb. In most situations, I find perspective first, then leverage of some kind, and then I change things. The biggest factor in finding that leverage is staying logical and non-emotional. So in this situation, how did I fix things? It was simple, actually. I started to charge a "this client is a pain in my ass" fee. Of course, that was not a line item actually appearing on the bill. There were, however, a few clients for whom I was tempted to actually list it on their final invoice before I played my favorite game called Fire the Client. The more difficult a client was to work with, the more I charged. If at any point the money wasn't worth it, I simply raised my prices.

This is not acting out of anger but out of logic. It is a simple equation of resources used. If every time I work for Client A I do the job, submit an invoice, and simply get paid on time, that process takes a certain amount of resources. If every time I do that same job for Client B I need to spend an extra hour on the phone fighting over the invoice, that takes more resources. If this is the pattern of Client B, they need to pay for the extra resources they are using. The bonus was that once Client B was paying for the extra resources, I never got mad about fighting with them on the phone. I was continuously reminding myself that they were literally paying me to fight with them. It's a great *policy to never tell a client no. Instead, tell them how much it's going to cost.*

Most people easily understand the concepts above. Don't let them get you upset. Stay profitable.

Feeling Good Exposes Vulnerability

People tend to have a more difficult time with the next concept. You are never allowed to let your happy feelings hurt you. Never get overexcited. You are most vulnerable when you have a smile on your face. You thought you were most vulnerable when you were feeling down? You weren't: feeling down is simply the result of being willing to try anything because you have nothing left to lose. If guided correctly, that position can actually be very powerful. **Remember that depression is just anger lacking enthusiasm in that moment.** Anger is one of the two most powerful motivating forces in a human.

A scared, hurt animal backed into a corner is very dangerous. A happy animal rolling onto its back, exposing its tummy because it expects you to rub it, is a very vulnerable animal.

The next time pride comes before a fall, pay attention to who is smiling right before things take a turn for the worse. Then pay attention to who is smiling after.

To summarize, do not give your power away by being emotional. Realize that most people you're going to deal with are emotional, so factoring that variable in is important. But the most important variable for everyone is still money, and this is how we keep score. Create win/win situations, and if someone feels bad in the process, apologize that they feel bad and stay on plan while you watch the scoreboard. Only apologize for your actions if they negatively affect the score. An organization that is competent and confident, and that knows how to communicate well, will always financially outperform an organization with "feeling good" as priority number one. When it comes to buying food and paying rent for their family, most people are willing to work jobs that they don't enjoy. However, when opportunity arises for that person to provide for their family *and* feel good, you watch them run to it. Understand the difference between the two, and know what angle to play from for any given situation.

Perspective

There is one last thing we need to cover before getting into the actual business methods. Before we can talk about solutions, we first need to define the problem. Exactly what problem are you trying to solve? This brings us to the very important topic of perspective. The perspective you choose defines the problem-solving process. If you focus on your feelings, they become a distraction and blind you from what truly needs to be done. When you can see things from a perspective free of emotion, the path to the solution becomes very clear and easy to follow.

We live in a society today that is more interested in feeling good about how they fail than they are in learning success. You need to understand that in any race second place is the first loser, and that it would be a shame for that person to not do whatever it takes to take it up a notch when they are so close to winning. **YOUR FEELINGS ARE IRRELEVANT TO THE PROCESS.** If you have been spending your entire life trying to convince yourself that "it's not that you lost, it's how you played the game," you should try success. If you have somehow convinced yourself to be happy with failure, think of the snow job you'll be able to do on yourself when you actually win!

A door-to-door door salesman has been selling doors for three months now. He has only one problem. He has never actually sold a door. He loves his work. He meets lots of new people every day. He spends a lot of his time outside, which is even better because he lives in Southern California. He never has had to deal with returns, replacements, or upset customers on the phone (mostly because he hasn't sold anything). He loves his job. After another week of this, however, his savings account at his bank is going to hit zero. At that point, he is going to start to feel bad about the fact that he is out of money.

Another man has been at his new job for three months now. He has been putting in an average of 10 hours of overtime per week in hopes of getting a quick promotion. One day he gets the nerve to walk into his boss's office and ask for the promotion. His boss agrees. His boss doesn't give him more money, as he explains that it is against the "rules" (that he just made up) to do that so soon, but he gives him the title of senior marketer and prints new business cards for him. His ego got stroked, and he is happy to work overtime for the next three months. Cost to the company: about $13.97 for the new business cards. This guy just fell victim to his own ego.

A third man who sells jet airplanes spills coffee on his biggest client right as he is about to sign an order for 10 of them. The man doesn't think about how dumb he should feel. He is focused on the commission check he is about to get. He apologizes for the accident, gets some paper towels to help clean up, and hands the client his pen back without missing a beat. The client knows that if he buys the planes from the man's competitor, he will end up paying about $970,000 more on the deal. The client doesn't even get upset about the coffee on his Fioravanti Power Look suit (real men wipe their asses with Armani). Both men are looking at the scoreboard and not paying much attention to anything else.

The correct questions are always "what did the client (**not** you) perceive?" and "how will it affect the scoreboard?" Did the client think you made a mistake? Maybe you didn't even do anything wrong but they still think so. You may have no clue how you offended them, but you did. Maybe you made a mistake that they don't care about. You need to put yourself in their position to figure out what needs fixing. This is why your feelings are irrelevant, because when it comes time to sign a check, the decision will be made based on a collection of their perceptions, not yours. How do they feel and/or what is their logic telling them? These are the correct questions. Focus on them.

Take yourself out of the equation for a second. See everything from third person. Look at the interaction and ask yourself how this person will tell the story of the interaction to others.

Think of your interactions like a movie you are starring in. Now place yourself in the theater watching this movie. As you watch yourself up on the screen interacting with others, you are in third person. You are watching yourself in the movie from outside of the movie. It is from this perspective that you will see and understand what's happening with the other characters much more clearly.

Remember, you are not allowed to say things like "they should have understood what you were trying to say" or that "they should have seen that you were only trying to help them." The ideas that they should have or could have, and your efforts of trying, do not factor in. People only consider their perceptions of the facts. For the purposes of what we are dealing with here, see it from their reality, even if you do not agree with how they see it.

Here is a simple way to figure out how they will tell the story of your interaction with others. Start with the five senses. What did they see, hear, touch, smell, and taste? This is how all of us collect information about our environment. Then ask yourself how they feel about the information they gathered. The best way to start guessing about how they feel is to know their belief system. The more you know about their belief system, the better you will be able to guess how they feel in any given situation. Are they environmentalists? Democrat or Republican? Are they religious? Did they grow up in a different country? Then imagine them telling the story to their girlfriend or wife. How would they tell the story to their boss, partner, or co-workers? Do everything you can to experience it through their reality. You now know what a real problem is and what is irrelevant. You know what needs to be fixed and more importantly what their definition of "fixed" is.

We now have you asking the correct questions and solving the correct problems, while ignoring the irrelevant. You are now ready to learn the actual business methods.

Value Is Perception

Anything that is the product of negotiation is negotiable. That is a very simple, completely true, and logically provable fact. Negotiation, by definition, is the mutual discussion and arrangement of the terms of a transaction or agreement. Everything in business is negotiable. Whenever anything goes wrong in business, you can negotiate, because you can always negotiate.

Speaking in the most basic terms, what happens when something goes wrong in business? The parties involved perceive a sudden and usually drastic change in value. Sometimes what went wrong left the other side perceiving a lower value for you and/or your product. Sometimes what went wrong is that you suddenly perceive, for whatever reason, that the other side has more value than you or your side. In either case, perception is of greater relevance than fact and never exactly equals fact. What someone accepts as fact cannot be arrived at without perception. It is not what is true or false, it is what a person perceives to be true or false. Perceptions are fluid and can at least be shaped, if not controlled, in any given situation.

I walk into a small electronics store to buy the newest gadget I read about last night. I love electronics. When it comes to technology, I am like a 10-year-old boy at Toys"R"Us. Anyway, I purchase my new toy and take it home to play with it. After a few minutes of fiddling with it and not being able to make it work, I arrive at the grand realization that I am not an imbecile. In fact, my new toy is broken.

I package it all back up, make a photocopy of my receipt, and drive back to the store. When I go to the counter and explain the problem, the person I am talking to points at a sign that reads, "No Refunds or Exchanges." I have just been told by a teenaged kid, who has yet to discover acne medication and deodorant, that I am stuck with my dead toy. He explains that it's simply the store's customer policy.

*I explain to him my purchasing policy. When I purchase an item, I expect it to actually work. We have now entered into a negotiation. I have my perspective, he has his, and the more powerful reality (*frame*) will win. Next I ask him if he has the authority to ignore that silly little rule of theirs. He tells me no and that he is just a part-time employee. I ask to talk to the owner. He hesitates, so it's time to adjust things again. I point at him and explain that he is an employee, which makes him overhead. I then point at myself and explain that I am a customer and represent revenue. He goes to get the owner.*

When the owner comes over, I start from scratch, explaining myself in a very matter-of-fact, non-emotional, logical way. The owner points at his sign, and I tell him about my purchasing policy. He doesn't budge, so it's time to adjust things with him. There are other customers in his store. Advantage me. Without getting emotional, I raise and project my voice so that his other customers can hear what I am about to say. I thank him, loudly, for being there after the sale to ensure my happiness with my purchase as I pat him on the back and wink at him. He is smart and knows exactly what I am doing. Keep in mind that at this point, I have actually helped the pending sales he currently has in his store (very important – create a win/win situation), but he knows that if he doesn't go along with it, I am the type of customer who will have no issue making a scene and killing those pending sales. I get my replacement. I go home and play with my new toy, joyfully.

How did it work? First, I stayed emotionless. Then I presented a win/win option. The owner chose the option that caused him the least trouble. Hold your reality separate from your emotions and don't let anyone divert you. The stronger reality always wins.

I have a friend who is a master of never paying full price. Sometimes it's a little annoying to be around. At other times it's just fun to watch. The last time we were in Las Vegas together, he negotiated with a cocktail waitress for free beer. It was possibly one of the most amusing things I have ever seen. Keep in mind that in Las Vegas of all places, the cocktail waitresses hear everything; they work in Sin City. Anyway, after my friend drinks his first Heineken, the waitress asks if he would like another. He says yes but asks if she is buying it and explains that it is only fair because he bought the first one. She cracks a smile, and I get popcorn for the show I know I am about to see. She answers no. He counter-offers at half price. She says that she cannot do that but guarantees that the next one will be extra cold. He asks if she has ever given free beer away. She says no. He says that if she brings him a free beer he will leave a $40 tip, and so she doesn't get in trouble, she can even ring it up at full price and just cover it out of her tip. She then looks at me and asks how much he has already had to drink. I explain that he is always like this. She rolls her eyes and goes to get his "free beer." While she is gone, I ask him if he realizes that in all actuality he paid more than everyone else who has ever purchased a Heineken at this bar. He was quick to correct me. He explained that he procured the second Heineken at *no cost, and the large tip was because the waitress was so willing to entertain him and play along. I didn't know how to argue with that.*

The last time this guy bought a car, he walked into a car dealership with an interesting reality. When the salesman asked if he was interested in buying a new car, he replied by responding no. He was there to "sell money" and asked if the salesman might be interested in possibly trading it for a car. It sounds a little funny, but guess who won that negotiation? My friend, whom no one could ever impose their reality on.

When things go wrong, do not dwell on where you are. Think of my friend and use this concept to get things moving and keep them moving in a positive direction.

The next time you are interviewing for a job, do not start off from a position of imbalanced value. Most people approach it from the idea that they are "asking for work." You are entering a negotiation, and so is your prospective employer. You each have something the other wants. This is a trade, not a favor for either side. Start off with the equation balanced, and keep the equation balanced. You may NEED a paycheck, but remember that you would not be there if they did not NEED the work done.

The Interrupt

When something goes wrong, people tend to focus on it. Obvious, I know. If I am on a plane and one of the engines catches fire, I am not focused on the other three that are still working properly. Another way to look at it is that if I focus on the mistakes others have made and call attention to them, I may be able to prevent others from seeing the mistakes I made. This is the *interrupt*, a derailment of thought and reassignment of focus.

Managers and bosses are typically masters of this. You know when you have fallen victim to this when you go in asking for a promotion and leave the boss's office almost empty-handed yet somehow feeling OK about it.

Salesmen are also very good at this. You go into an appliance wholesaler to buy a new refrigerator. You know exactly what you want and how much you are willing to pay for it. Somehow you leave paying $300 over your budget for a feature you did not initially want.

The above two examples are what happens when the *interrupt* is used in a win/loss environment. For the technique to work, the person using it has to interrupt and then play your emotions. How do you protect yourself from the *interrupt*? Do not fall into their reality, stay logical, and give them no emotion to play. Now that you know how to protect yourself from the misuse of this in win/lose situations, let's learn how you can apply it in win/win situations.

From whatever perspective people are seeing things at any given moment, there is always a bigger picture, and there are always smaller details. People who focus only on the big picture tend to miss the details that can lead to the death of the project. People who focus only on the details tend to forget the goal of the project and never get anywhere. When things start falling off of the track, sometimes the only way to get them back on track is to either go up a level to gain perspective or drill down to details to find the cause.

Remember my computer consulting company? One of its clients was a large provider of natural gas refueling facilities. They had stations all over the U.S. and Canada. My company had a contract with them to manage their technology infrastructure. Remember I told you that on a big enough scale, things go wrong? This was a big scale, things went wrong, and when they did, it cost the company a lot of money. My company could not keep things 100% and do it 100% of the time. No company could. My company was in there because it did a better job than anyone else could at the time.

The point of this story however isn't that. The fun part of this story is that the head of this company and the owner of the technology company they depended on (me) did not get along, at all, ever. He was like a low-budget, dumber version of Donald Trump, with less of a sense of humor. He thought I was an egomaniac with a general lack of respect for everyone. Looking back to that time, I would say we were both correct. Anyway, we learned to just avoid each other. I made very good money, and they had a great technology infrastructure. Why complicate it and ruin a good thing? We both knew that.

Sometimes the *interrupt* is not used to define the current situation. Sometimes the *interrupt* is used over time, as in the next example.

Gordon is 20 years old. He is 5-foot-11 and weighs about 145 pounds. Gordon has made a decision. Gordon has decided that he wants to have the physique of a person who unmistakably lifts weights. He has never lifted weights before in his life, so he has some work ahead of him.

*As Gordon enters the gym for the first time, people laugh at him. He is smart enough to ignore it. While working out during his first day, he talks to a few of the people in better shape who are working out next to him. He finds out that most of the guys who look like he wants to look have their workouts about four days a week for a little more than one hour each time. Gordon reaches a logical conclusion. If he continues to work out for long enough at a rate of five days per week for one and a half hours each day, he will look at least as good as the people he was talking to. He is not completely correct, however. The factor he left out was that he would also need to learn **how** to work out. Interestingly enough, this problem actually solves itself. When the people who are at the gym all the time start to recognize Gordon as a regular and see his commitment, they help teach him how to improve his workouts. In the years following, Gordon gets many more dates because he had the willpower to "interrupt" the mockery of others as he exuded focus and drive toward his goal.*

In business, it's similar: you do not have to let anyone get you down by saying that you're a small company. You begin by acting like a big company, and in time you become a big company. If you listen to those who call you a small company, you can never become a big company. You have to *interrupt* what they say now with what you will be tomorrow. Act as if you are on your way to achieving your goals because in fact you are; you prove this by your action. When they laugh at you, you know that as time passes, they will have less to laugh about. If you really want to piss these people off, succeed. Not only is this the best revenge, but it is also the only type of revenge you can get without throwing negative energy into the universe.

A man's boss storms into his office. He is upset because the man just missed the weekly staff meeting. The topic of the meeting was how to increase slumping sales. The man explains that he just got off a phone call where he completed a large order. The signed purchase order is sitting on his fax machine next to him.

People tend to think about what is in front of them. Change what they are focused on and you change how they feel. Be sure you are focusing on the right thing. Keep others focused on the right thing. It's the right thing when everyone wins.

Gaps of Understanding

In Social Basics we called this section Perceptual Flexibility. In Business Basics, we call it Gaps of Understanding. In a social situation, it is perfectly acceptable to tease people and have fun with them. Remember the following example as a girl is trying to get away from you by running to the bar.

She says: I'm thirsty... I think I want a drink.
He says: Oh, thank you. Um, Heineken for me, please.

Or maybe she was trying to get you to buy her a drink. Either way, it doesn't matter. We may not necessarily have her best interests in mind, but it's just a beer. You are having fun, and if you are doing it right, she is smiling, thus having fun also. In business, we assume you are working from a reality of a win/win situation. The rule is that if you think there may be a difference between what you assume and what they assume, you should err on the side of the positive. Give them the option of either agreeing or correcting you. Understand their needs. Have their best interests in mind. Then assume the sale.

Client: I will be able to review the final contract
                by the end of the day tomorrow.
Salesman: Perfect. I can stop by the following
                morning to pick up the signed documents
                or answer any final questions you may
                have before signing. How about
                10:00 AM?

The other application of this method is to ask questions with your desired answer included.

After wasting 30 minutes of the salesperson's time, I inquire, "If I were to buy this suit today, would it come with a free tie?"

When an employee tells me that I am sure to love the proposal he has guaranteed to get to me by 4:30 Friday, I tell him I hope so because it would be a shame if he had to work over the weekend fixing anything he missed.

This is the power of suggestion at work. When you start using this method, you will be amazed how often it works to your benefit. Whenever there exists a gap in understanding, you fill it in. Given the option between your reality and someone else's, always choose yours. You will be surprised how often people will go with the first idea that is proposed simply because they either don't want to fight it or don't want to have to come up with their own idea. **The lazy and uncertain will ALWAYS yield to those who are in a state of action toward what they have decided they will have.**

Domination Basics Part 3
Power Basics

You pulled it off. You find yourself sitting at one of New York's finest restaurants for dinner with one of New York's finest women. Her name is Cynthia, and she is a part-time model in her second year of law school. You met each other three weeks ago on a beach in Miami when you walked up to her and told her that you liked her smile. It turned out to be the best night of your life. As you were saying your goodbyes, she asked you to meet her for dinner in New York to continue the adventure.

Getting to where you are now, sitting across from this amazing woman who is looking warmly into your eyes, was no small feat. In fact, you find yourself here by a slight stretch of the truth. You may have led her to believe that you're cooler than you actually are. Hell, let's be honest: she's completely out of your league, and that's why you have such a big smile on your face right now. It's not the slight stretch of the truth that's about to bite you in the ass, it's the more-than-slight stretch of your financial resources that it took to get here.

It's when she orders dessert that the thought first crosses your mind: "I hope I have enough left on my credit card to cover the addition of dessert." Ah, you're probably fine.

After paying for the flight out, the nice hotel you're hoping to take her back to after dinner, and the unexpected extra hold they put on your credit card at the car rental place (you never rented a Porsche before), you know you're tight. You're fine with all that because this girl is amazing. That's when it happens. The waiter returns to your table and gives you a strange look that causes a sinking sensation in your stomach.

"I'm sorry sir, your card didn't go through."

You begin to sweat as Cynthia looks at you. Two seconds of silence feels like an eternity of your very soul being on fire. Your brain searches frantically for options to save your dignity and keep the hope alive of a relationship with this girl. Is there some rabbit that can be pulled out of your hat?

Nope. You're fucked!

Not every story has a happy ending. I may be unusually skilled at applying social lubricant, but I've learned the hard way that if you don't understand the dangers of the toys you're playing with, you can really hurt yourself. The concepts presented here in Power Basics **MUST** be your guide on your rise to power. My material isn't written for the 12-year-old who wants to be the coolest kid on his block. My material is written for men who are hell-bent on winning every game they play in life as they ultimately risk it all to get it all. For people who will play the game to its limits, what I am about to tell you is information that will save your life.

If you think I'm being overly dramatic here, I ask the following question: What are the two biggest reasons for both murder and suicide? Money and women.

Even though we may have never met, I know you better than you realize. By the very nature of you reading this, I know that I just named two of the three things you seek, money and women. The third thing is power. I'm about to show you the nature of how these three things interact with one another, and then I'm going to teach you how to use this knowledge to ultimately build a never-ending supply of all of them.

Money, Women, and Power

"In this country, you gotta make the money first.
Then when you get the money, you get the power.
Then when you get the power, then you get the
women."

> *- Tony Montana (gangster)*
> *From the movie "Scarface"*

"See I believe in money, power and respect
First you the money
Then you get the motherfuckin' power
And after you get the fuckin' power
You get the fuckin' niggaz to respect you"

> *- Lil' Kim (rapper)*
> *Lyrics from "Money, Power, Respect"*

As much as I respect the energy and conviction of the two above quotations, they are both unfortunately wrong. Look at the world around you and you will see every guy chasing money, women, and power. I remember someone telling me once to never trust a skinny pastry chef. If 99% of the guys on the planet are going after money, women, and power, and they don't have it, it should be obvious that their methods are flawed.

The logic of the masses is that you need money to buy goods and services. Get money, and you will have what you need to "get things done." As you're using money to move forward on your plans, you can enjoy some of this money as you buy yourself things like designer clothes, huge houses, exotic cars, and expensive dinners. This is when you start to feel like a real man. Next, as the money buys the lifestyle, women become attracted to you. As you drive around town in your exotic sports car with your model girlfriend in the passenger seat, that's when you feel power. At this point, you're not going to take shit from anyone because they all want what you have. This is how the masses think you gain money, women, and power, by doing it in that order. Wrong!

> *Jason is sitting on a bench, waiting for a bus. The light turns red and a convertible Lamborghini pulls up. One of the hottest women he has ever seen is in the passenger seat. As he looks at the guy driving, he thinks to himself, "If I had a car like that, I could have a woman like that."*

Jason is thinking like the masses and, like them, is completely wrong. He never considers that the car and woman are both results of this guy's inner power. In other words, the woman isn't attracted to the car; she is attracted to this guy's core power, which is also why he has this car. It's inherent that a guy with this much internal power will make the ridiculous amounts of money needed to live like this. People get the cause and effect backwards. This guy has real inner power which naturally results in the money, and then the women.

External Validation

So why is it that everyone has this backwards in their heads? People for the most part believe they are weak. They have been conditioned by society to think that if they have nothing, they are nothing. This is how external validation works. The more stuff you have, the more power you feel you have. Power behaves in a strange way. If you feel as if you have it, you do. If you don't feel as if you have it, it escapes you. For most men, possessions make them feel as if they have power.

Give a guy the corner office, a new BMW, put him in an Armani suit, and he will feel like a somebody. Take him to the beach that weekend and a magical thing happens. All of a sudden, he is way more popular with the ladies. Now consider the insanity of this for a moment. The women he is talking with have no knowledge of his suit (because he is in a swimsuit), they know nothing about the car he drove there, and they know nothing about his job. But somehow, his having this stuff makes him better with the ladies! Here is the most interesting part. If he starts talking about this stuff (letting the girls know about the things that make him feel powerful), it will only backfire on him and make him look like a pompous jackass.

So you see in this example, the physical items don't affect the *women*; the physical items affect the *guy*. Change the guy's state through external validation, and he feels powerful. The women are attracted to the guy feeling powerful.

The first problem with this model is the obvious. If he loses the items, his power vanishes also. The second problem is a bit better hidden. The second problem is, without power in the first place, what is he using to get the money? I'm sure you have heard the saying "it takes money to make money." That's also completely wrong. It takes *power* to make money, and after that, you can use both power and money to make more money.

Power, Money, and then Women

Some of the best examples I know of the concepts I'm presenting here are in the move *The Usual Suspects* (1995). If ever there was a character who summed up what you are learning here, it's Keyser Söze. I strongly recommend seeing this movie.

> *"They realized that to be in power, you didn't need guns or money or even numbers. You just needed the will to do what the other guy wouldn't."*
> *- Verbal Kint*

Everything starts with gaining power, then money, and then women. This is the order in which things must be done. If you get this in the wrong order, your life will turn into disaster. This knowledge may become a very hard pill to swallow as you read further and discover all of its implications, but it's the truth.

One of the reasons that the masses resist the idea of power first is social conditioning. Popular television, movies, and songs have been hypnotizing you your entire life to believe that it's money, women, and then power. As I said, you cannot win with this approach, and that is exactly why those in power have been feeding you this wrong information. Why, you ask?

Their two reasons are a desire to stay in power and a desire to have you as their volunteered slaves.

People in power always fear losing their power. People without power will always look for power. It's difficult for the powerful to convince the weak that they don't want power. The easy solution is for the powerful to manipulate the weak into chasing their tails. The powerful "help" the weak with the wrong advice. The powerful convince the weak that to get power, you must first get money. If you convince the weak that they need money before they can have power, you ensure three things. The first is that the weak will never be able to actually gain much money, because in reality they must first gain power to gain any real amount of money. The second is that because the recipe for power the weak are following doesn't work, the weak will never actually gain any real power. The powerful thereby guarantee that the weak will never accumulate enough power to overthrow them (or steal their women). But wait, it gets better. The third thing is that by convincing the mass population that they need money before they can have anything else, the powerful turn that population into slaves. Because the powerful have true power, money becomes an easily renewable resource for them. They then give money to the population to carry out their plans and thereby increase their power. It's misdirection as the masses chase money, believing it will get them power, but all the while the process is actually preventing them from gaining any substantial amount of either. Welcome to the reality no one sees! As long as you are thinking money, women, and power, you are on a hamster wheel, a race without a finish line.

You must accept the hidden true reality and jump off the hamster wheel. Other than the lifetime of social conditioning, one other factor will make accepting this difficult. Consider for a moment what this all means. If money and women automatically come to those with power, what prevents you from gaining power?

Are you ready for this one? Nothing. There is no person, no object, and no limit of physical reality that prevents it. It's 100% in your head. To understand this is to realize that all power is a gift from the weak. **<u>ALL POWER IS A GIFT FROM THE WEAK!</u>** All power, 100% of it. Next, realize that because of this, there is no such thing as "gaining power." That's not how power works. What you hold in your head as the concept of gaining power is simply nothing more than not giving your power away. All power is a gift from the weak.

As you start to fully digest the implications of this, you, like most people, will become very unsettled and fight this reality. If the truth is that no thing and no one stands in your way, you become forced to admit that you are the only reason that you don't have power.

You are your own worst enemy. Nothing is stopping you other than yourself, and if you accept this fact and take action on it, the money and women will very easily and quickly follow. It's in our human nature to blame others and to deceive ourselves into thinking that outside forces are working against us. Living in an "I can't" world is easy. Coming to terms with the reality that we actually live in an "I can but I choose not to out of fear and laziness" world, now that's a real bitch. As you begin to understand what you have just read, you will find this to be the most difficult and most empowering concept you will ever face in life.

If You Gain Money Before Power

Let's look at what happens when you get money before power. The basic problem here is that money before power is like handing the cure for cancer to a two-year-old written on the back of a napkin, which the kid puts in its mouth and then chokes to death on. The first thing you need to understand about money is that money is only a tool. Some say that money brings happiness while others disagree. The reality of money is that it will simply bring the person who gets it more of what they already had before they had money. Give money to a person with stress in their lives, and it will buy them more stress. Give money to an unhappy person, and they will become more unhappy. Give money to someone with an already happy and fulfilling life, and you can watch the smile on their face get even bigger. If you introduce me to a person about to receive 10 million dollars and ask me how that money is going to affect their lives, six months later you'd think I was a fortune-teller. It will simply buy them more of what they already had. This is the reason for the most incredible statistic that people on welfare who win the lottery quickly end up broke and right back to where they started. Money wasn't the problem. Their ability to manage money was, is, and probably always will be a problem for them. This is why if you give them money, it just escapes them, yet again.

You Need Power Before Money

Place a samurai sword in the hands of a master and you'll be amazed at what he can do. A man like this on the dark path can do much harm as easily as a man like this on the light path can do much good. The sword can be used to destroy or protect, all depending on the hand that holds it. Place that sword in the hands of a baby and it will never be lifted off of the ground to do either. You now understand that it's not the sword but the hand that holds it. If it were the sword, a baby could defend itself from a samurai warrior simply by having the same sword.

Money is like a sword. Power is in the hand that holds it. If you think you can simply use money to cut through all your problems, you are wrong. First you must train your hand to use the sword.

In the rap and hip-hop community, they say that "game recognize game." It doesn't matter how much money you have because if you don't know how to run it, if you don't have game, you will instantly be recognized as a fake and treated as such. In the hood, that equates to "the thugs jackin' yo shit, dog!"

It is said that a fool and his money are easily parted. Money has a way of moving toward the most powerful person in the room. You may think that the money has a tendency to move toward those who already have the money, but what you are really seeing is nothing more than the powerful with a head start. Change the way you look at the game, and notice that the game changes for you.

The Money Smokescreen

The reason people are so unhappy is that they get so engrossed with the idea of getting money that they forget what they wanted money for. My next story illustrates how lost people have become.

I walk into a hardware store, ready for my next live social experiment. I see a man looking at drills. I ask him if he is thinking about buying a drill. He says yes, and I ask if he is sure it's a drill that he really wants. He gives me a strange look and tells me that in fact, yes, it is a drill that he wants. I tell him that I don't think he wants a drill, but I think I know what he really wants. He now gives me an annoyed look and says, "Yeah, what's that?" I go on to explain to him that he doesn't want a drill, and I know this because no one who buys a drill actually wants a drill. They actually want a hole. What if you could have the hole without a drill?

Money has a tendency to create a smokescreen that makes you forget what you actually want. Not many people consider that they can have the hole without the drill. Seek the hole (no pun intended) and not the drill, my friends. When it is the hole that you focus on, you begin to see other options that you did not notice before that will give you the hole.

Before my twentieth birthday, I was earning enough money to afford a move up into the very prestigious and very rich hills of Newport Beach, California. I laughed hysterically at most of my neighbors every day. Most people got up very early to drive down the hill to their office and didn't return until hours after sunset. Once they got home, they were so exhausted that they ate dinner and went right to bed. During the day, my neighborhood was a deserted ghost town, and during the night, no one was awake. I was surrounded by gorgeous parks, trails, pools, and clubhouses that no one but me and my friends ever used. Everyone was working so hard to have these things that they never had the time or energy to enjoy them. Before I moved up onto the hill, I used to look up at the houses and want to be up there. I had this in common with my neighbors after they moved in. My neighbors would look up to the hill from their jobs down below at the houses they owned and wish they were up there. I eventually left those hills. It was a very boring and lonely place.

Be very careful not to become like one of my neighbors. They were so focused on getting just a little more that they enjoyed nothing.

A friend of mine once took two trips to Europe when he was young and had zero money. He tells me that if he had focused on saving up to pay for it (focused on money), he would have never been able to go. He discovered instead that if he took 20 people with him and played tour guide, he could not only go for free, but he would even make some money in the process. As I said, he went twice.

Focus on the hole. Think of it as focusing on the prize while ignoring society's rules on how you are supposed to get it. Do this, let the options show themselves to you, and you'll discover that you can win prizes you previously thought to be out of your reach.

The Magician's Bank Account

You would think that only a magician could have nothing in the bank (as far as the IRS is concerned) yet at the same time all of the money they could ever spend to buy things. This is exactly how the bank accounts of the world's most powerful people are, and yes, it's just like magic.

> *Money only seems real in small amounts. If you haven't eaten in a few days and someone gives you $10, that money seems real because it buys you food. Get paid $10 per hour and work for 100 hours digging ditches, and that $1,000 seems real also. Do a business deal on paper, deposit a six-figure check into your bank account, and it all seems like Monopoly money. Spend that Monopoly money on a car, and somehow it doesn't really feel like your car. Speaking as someone who has deposited his share of six-figure checks and experienced more than his share of what they call "easy come, easy go," I can tell you that it is like living in a fantasy world, all paid for with fantasy money.*

Truly wealthy people don't pursue money. To them, it's all Monopoly money, simply used to keep score in the games they play. Truly wealthy people pursue power. When you make the rules of the game, manipulating the score is very easy. The powerful don't care about owning things; they want to control things. It's not about having money, it's about controlling the money of a shell company. When you own something, it can be taken away from you and/or used against you. When you truly control something, you have all the benefits without any of the headaches.

The next thing you will discover is that when you have the power, people will volunteer their money to you. Taken to the extreme, a cult leader has nothing but power, and his followers will offer him everything, including their lives. With enough power, the world is given to you. Power is a gift from the weak.

Lessons from a Pimp

A true pimp isn't the most handsome guy or the wealthiest guy, but he has the power and knows how to use it to make money. The important thing to realize is that he was a pimp before he made the money; he didn't make the money and then become a pimp. He was always a pimp. What makes him a pimp is his power over women.

How Women Prevent the Accumulation of Money

Larry and Doug just graduated from high school. They're roommates, and both are waiting a year before deciding if they will attend college or not. They have full-time jobs at the same electronics store. After paying all their monthly bills, each has $350 left over. This is where the similarities stop. Larry has a girlfriend. Doug is single. Over the next year, Larry will spend 20 hours a week and $350 per month with his girlfriend. Doug will spend 20 hours a week and $350 per month starting a business. At the end of the year, that will total 1,040 hours and $4,200 for each of them.

After a year, Larry hasn't signed up for college, and his girlfriend dumps him. She thinks he's a loser with no ambition in a dead-end job. Life is very different for Doug. His business really took off, and he isn't working at the electronics store anymore. Doug also decides not to go to college but for very different reasons. He's making a little over $90,000 a year at age 19 and only working 30 hours a week now because his employees do most of the work. Care to guess *where Larry's ex-girlfriend is? She is going to Spain this weekend with Doug.*

After returning from Spain, Doug becomes a Larry. Doug focuses his attention on his new girlfriend and starts to spend all of his extra money on extravagant trips around the world. As it was with Larry, Doug's girlfriend leaves him after a year for a guy she met in Aspen, Colorado, a trip Doug paid for. She tells Doug that somewhere he lost that entrepreneurial passion that attracted her to him in the first place. Doug gets very depressed and loses what little interest he had left in his business. This leaves Doug with his money spent and his passion gone, and without his passion, he will never make the money back. He sees himself as just another failed entrepreneur getting a two-year late start at college. This is the very common story of "the loser that could have been a multimillionaire."

Nothing will prevent the accumulation of money like a woman. Show me a young man destined to be a great entrepreneur, add one gorgeous woman, and at the point she becomes his girlfriend, his financial potential will dwindle to a small fraction of what it could have been. Money spent with a woman is **_NEVER_** an investment, it is an expense. Being with the right woman is an awesome feeling, but money spent on that woman is **_NEVER_** something on which you will see a financial return. Simple economics tells us that the lower our expenses and the more we invest, the more money we will accumulate.

So am I telling you to not get into a serious relationship until you build up your bank account? Yes, exactly! Hang out with women, enjoy spending time together, have a lot of sex, but don't get into a serious relationship until you build the foundation of your empire. Break this rule and no empire for you. It's just that simple. The other thing you need to keep in mind is that you need practice being with women, many women and much practice, before you will even be ready for a real relationship with one of the planet's most desirable women. You are spending your time now building up money and learning how to attract women so that later on, you're a multimillionaire with a supermodel girlfriend half your age. If you let the first mediocre girl willing to have sex with you get you into a relationship, none of this will ever happen.

This demonstrates how a woman can prevent the accumulation of money. You spend money on them (expense) that you should be using for building your financial future (investment). You also spend time with them that you should be using for building your financial future. There are only so many hours in the day. The last thing you must factor in is the limited amount of emotional energy you have. This is the source of your passion and the raw energy from which your empire will take its shape. Friedrich Nietzsche said that having a woman in your life makes the highs higher and the lows more frequent. He was correct. Try working on marketing material for your new business after a fight with your girlfriend and you will see what I'm talking about. If you live with her, it will be even worse. Her idea of a committed relationship is that no matter how shitty she is acting or feeling, you're stuck experiencing all of it with her. This is not something you can financially afford at this point in your life.

Find some self-sufficient girls to hang out with who don't need money from you to pay for the lifestyles they want but can't afford *AND* who don't need to be someone's girlfriend to feel as if they have stability and self-worth *AND* who don't use you like an emotional dumpster as they expect you to help fix their problems.

They may be harder to find, but you and your future are worth it! Again, you will never find women like this if you end up being the boyfriend of the first mediocre girl who was willing to sleep with you. You tell them that you're "just not boyfriend material right now." It's 100% true, and the best part is that the more you push them away, the more they will chase you.

Disconnecting the Cash from the Vagina

Guys think that if they have money, women will follow them around, but in reality the women won't be following them around. The women will be following the money around. If you want to own a woman's mind, body, and soul, you need to understand that no amount of money can buy them. Money has a tendency to "rent" women, either over the short term, like a prostitute, or over the long term, like a divorced wife. Truly possessing a woman mind, body, and soul can only be done with power.

Phillip pays a prostitute $500 for sex, and as soon as it's over, she jumps out of bed. As she's putting her clothes back on, Phillip says, "But wait, I want you to stay." She tells him it will cost another $500 for her to stay. Phillip is out of money, and she is out the door off to take the next guy's money. Ten minutes later, he can hear her having sex in the motel room next door. This is just like the story of Larry and Doug, the kind of thing that can really mess with a guy's head. This is not the kind of thing that men really want.

Gwen cannot help but approach Enrique at the bar. He has that look of unshakeable confidence. Like all women, she finds power to be the sexiest quality a man can have. Ten minutes later, they are leaving for his apartment. As soon as the door shuts, she jumps on him and screws his balls off. Once it's finally over and even the ceiling is wet with the remnants of passion, she is asking when she can see him again. She begs, "Let me come over tomorrow and cook you dinner baby." This is what men truly want. You don't get that from money, you get that from power.

Guys need to stop thinking that they need money to get women, because they are way overcomplicating things. Sex is a natural thing. Most guys approach sex with the attitude that they are attempting to do the impossible, as if it is the most unnatural thing in the universe. Are you kidding me? It's necessary for the very survival of the human race. It doesn't get any more natural than that! We need to get back to basics. We are all here today because yesterday, and the day before, and 100 years before that, and 10,000 years before that, everyone's been having sex. The idea of you and a girl having sex is a completely natural thing that's been going on since the beginning of our species. The unnatural concept that was introduced later on is money.

There are certain times when I am *especially* proud of my 100% German heritage. This is the case with the German band Rammstein. You may remember a song from 1997 titled *Du Hast* by them. It was used on the soundtrack for the original *Matrix* movie. Much energy, I love it. In 2009 they released another song simply titled *Pussy*. I recommend downloading the mostly-English version of the video (the mp3 won't do it justice). Be sure to get the unedited, uncensored, X-rated version and be sure that there aren't any children around. As you watch it, you're going to find yourself either completely uncomfortable or completely amused, or possibly both, as I was. Anyway, the part of the song I wanted to call attention to is where he says, "You've got a pussy. I have a dick. So what's the problem? Let's do it quick." This video may be beyond crude, but I think that in its mockery of today's uptight society, it makes a good point. Human sexuality should be approached like a trip to the amusement park with a friend, not something dark, shameful, and overcomplicated. There is something very wrong if you need to bribe your friend to come enjoy the amusement park with you.

Building Your Power

The core metaphor that I use to navigate the planet is as follows:

I'm in a great mood because as far as I'm concerned, life's a party. I find myself standing next to someone, and as I always do, I strike up a conversation with them. I say, "It's a nice day out." They uncomfortably reply with, "No it's not! It's raining." I'm talking to an insane person, because there isn't a cloud in the sky. That's when the person standing next to them says, "Hold me, I'm scared of thunder and lightning." That's when I walk away from the two insane people. I say to the next person I meet, "It's a nice day out." That person looks up at the sky, then back at me smiling and says, "Yes, it is a nice day out." Oh goodie! I found another person like me who gets it.

As I walk the planet, I meet so many people who are insane and are convinced otherwise simply because they are surrounded by other insane people. As you separate yourself from the masses, your new perspective will show you just how insane they are behaving. Social conditioning makes people think, and then do, amazingly silly things.

In the movie/mini-series *Roots* (1977), there is a scene where Kunta Kinte (the African) becomes Toby (the slave). In that scene, as soon as Kunta Kinte arrives in America, he is asked his name. He replies with "Kunta Kinte" and gets a few lashings with a whip. He is then told his name is Toby by the person holding the whip, who then asks him his name again. He replies with "Kunta Kinte" and receives a few more lashings with the whip. This continues until he is bloodied and finally replies with "my name is Toby." For every client I work with, at the heart of his issues is the fact that he became "Tobified." It's just a question of who did it and what they used as a whip. This is how social conditioning won its power over you.

> *Take a toddler out to a public place, and they have no inhibitions as they run up to strangers and pull on their clothes while saying, "Hello, I'm Kunta Kinte." That child will treat every person the same, man or woman, attractive or ugly, rich or poor. At some point, social conditioning kills that in us.*

> *A young man walks up to a girl at a bar and says, "Hello, I'm Kunta Kinte." The woman looks at him in disagreement and says, "No, your name is bitch, and you're going to buy me a drink!" (Whipisssh!) This happens a few times, and he becomes self-conscious and uncomfortable. He becomes Tobified. This is why most men walk up*

*to women and say, "Hello, I'm Toby. Can I buy
you a drink?"*

*My goal is to get men to remember that they
are men. During live coaching, my clients get all
riled up and excited that yes, in fact they are men!
They get a smile out of me as we walk into a bar
and they tell me that they truly believe women are
lucky to be talking to them. Then they see a cute
girl, walk up to her, and say, "Hello, I'm Toby.
Can I buy you a drink?" This will repeat a few
times until I can get them to walk up to a woman
and simply say, "Hello, I'm Kunta Kinte, and I
came over here to flirt with you." The first time it
works, they remember that in fact they were born a
real man. Whether it be women at a bar, other
guys at the gym, or people they work with, it's all
the same thing.*

You are a real man who has been conditioned like
an elephant.

*Go to a circus and look at baby elephants that
have been tethered. They use dramatically big
stakes in the ground to ensure that the baby
elephant cannot escape. Look at an adult elephant
that has been tethered and be amazed that the stake
in the ground is so small even though the adult
elephant is much bigger. As a baby, that elephant*

*learned that it could not pull the stake out of the
ground, so it gave up. As an adult, as soon as it
feels the tension in the rope, it gives up. If that
adult elephant would ignore the tension and give it
a good pull, that elephant would be free.*

What was your name again? Ignore the tension
and pull yourself free! I can't pull that stake out of the
ground for you. Well, I could, meaning that I am
physically able to, but if I do that, you will just look at
me as if I have some power you don't. You need to do
it yourself and thereby discover your own power. My
job is to simply remind you that it's possible, and guide
you when you're ready to set yourself free.

Give a bag of peanuts to an elephant ready to pull
his stake out of the ground, and he will do nothing
except eat the peanuts. The biggest problem you're
going to have with the process of setting yourself free is
distraction. When you let people divert your focus, you
give them your power. When you let other people's
emotional state affect your emotional state, you give
them your power. You must separate yourself from the
insanity of those surrounding you. Don't let anything
distract you from pulling your stake out of the ground.
Remember, there is no person, no object, and no limit
of physical reality that prevents it. It's 100% in your
head.

Once you do set yourself free, you will be like an elephant standing in Central Park with a confused look on your face best described as "what do I do now?" This is the time to deal with your fears, because it is fear that makes us give our power away. Power is a gift from the weak that is given out of fear. To build up your power, you must expunge your reasons for giving it away.

All your fears fit into one of three categories. The first category is for things involving a statistically high physical risk. This is the category for a fear of walking into a lion cage at the zoo, pulling a gun on a police officer, and jumping out of a plane without a parachute. The second category is for things involving high financial costs. Swimming with sharks for 45 minutes off of the coast in the Bahamas is a relatively safe way to remind yourself you're alive, but it's too expensive for most people. Because the first category will get you killed and the second category may require finances that you don't have, we will focus on the third category. Coincidentally, when you fully deal with the third category, your fears in the first and second categories will vanish. OK, so what is this third category?

The third category is where we file all your fears that don't directly involve lethal physical danger or spending money you don't have. These are things like participating at a fully nude beach, walking up to an attractive woman and saying hello, and singing along

121

with your mp3 player in public as if you're the only person on the planet. It's the things that you are scared of doing simply because at some point, you decided to give your power away in these situations. There is no physical or monetary risk, yet you behave as if you are risking something tangible. You are just being a pussy.

Why is it that when I ask students to approach attractive women, half of them look at me like I'm completely crazy? It's as if I were asking them to put their junk under a pickle slicer that's in the hands of a man-hating lesbian bull-dyke. I have never had a client fall victim to a bizarre castration accident as a result of approaching an attractive woman.

At some point you will need to see your irrational fears for what they are, which is irrational, and push past them. Take the advice of Nike and "Just do it!" Realize as you do that you're not actually risking anything real. That's where you will find your power. It's time to become a man, to face your fears, and realize that it's all shadows in the mist.

Rent *The Usual Suspects* and then re-read the Power Basics section. These words will appear differently right after watching it. You will then understand that your ego is nothing more than the fear of being weak. Do not be afraid to be weak. Never be too proud to become strong. Be like Keyser Söze.

There is no person, no object, and no limit of physical reality that prevents you from having power. Deal with your fears and the power will be yours, as it always was, before you gave it away. First you get the power, then you build up the money, and then you get the women. Start by finding the power, the money and women will find you.

My name is Drawk Kwast, and my time on this planet has turned into quite the adventure. I've been slapped, I've been sued, and I've made myself look like a raging idiot on more than one occasion, but at least it's always been exciting. I have paid the price to learn what others will never know and to gain what others will never have. I've experienced the thrill of winning games that few have the balls to even play.

Remember, in every generation there are two groups. Now that you've made your choice, it's time to live it…

www.drawkkwast.com/book2

Acknowledgments

Publishing a book is a real pain in the ass, especially if it's your first one, as this was mine. I could fill quite a few pages by listing everyone who influenced this work, from other authors I've read, teachers I've learned from, people I've pissed off, and women I've pleasured. If I've ever slept on your couch, or with your sister/daughter/wife, or if we've somehow exchanged money or laughter, this is my official thank you. The life I've lived has required many interesting people to make it what it is.

That being said, the following people and companies deserve recognition for their help in the final production of this book.

Shelton Keith Hill - Conceptual Proofreading

Mike Murray - Conceptual Proofreading

Chazz Layne - Layout & Graphic Design

Dave Peyton - Proofreading

ProofreadingPal.com - Final Proofreading

CreateSpace.com - Printing & Distribution

What to Do Next

You have just read *Domination Basics: Secrets of the Alpha Male Book 1.* Go to my website at **www.drawkkwast.com** to get the next book in the series, *Power Communication: Secrets of the Alpha Male Book 2.* While you're at my website, you can check out my blog, sign up for my newsletter, and if you're really serious about getting your shit together, have a look at Total Experience Immersion, listed under my training programs.